Carolina North

Ordinances Passed by the State Convention

at its Second Adjourned Session

Carolina North

Ordinances Passed by the State Convention
at its Second Adjourned Session

ISBN/EAN: 9783744794213

Printed in Europe, USA, Canada, Australia, Japan

Cover: Foto ©Suzi / pixelio.de

More available books at **www.hansebooks.com**

Ordered to be Printed.

John W. Syme, Printer to the Convention.

ORDINANCES PASSED BY THE STATE CONVENTION AT ITS SECOND ADJOURNED SESSION.

[No. 1.]

AN ORDINANCE TO AUTHORIZE THE GOVERNOR TO EMBODY THE MILITIA FOR THE DEFENCE OF THE STATE.

Be it ordained by the Delegates of the people of North Carolina, in Convention assembled, and it is hereby ordained by the authority of the same, That for the emergency mentioned in his message of to-day, the Governor of the State is hereby authorized to order out such portions of the militia, as he may deem necessary to repel the invasion of the State.

Read three times and passed on the 21st day of Jan., 1862.

W. N. EDWARDS,

Pres. of Convention.

Teste:

WALTER L. STEELE, Secretary,

L. C. EDWARDS, Assistant Secretary.

[No. 2.]

AN ORDINANCE TO MODIFY AND PERFECT AN ORDINANCE PASSED AT THE LAST SESSION OF THE CONVENTION, ENTITLED "AN ORDINANCE

TO PROVIDE FOR THE RAISING OF MONEY FOR
THE SUPPORT OF GOVERNMENT, AND FOR THE
ISSUE OF TREASURY NOTES FOR THE PURPOSE
OF PAYING THE PUBLIC DEBT AND PURCHAS-
ING SUPPLIES FOR THE MILITARY FORCES EM-
PLOYED FOR DEFENCE IN THE PRESENT WAR,
AND FOR OTHER PURPOSES."

1. *Be it ordained by the delegates of the people of North
Carolina, in Convention assembled, and it is hereby ordained by
the authority of the same,* That so much of the ordinance passed
at the last session of this Convention, entitled "An Ordinance
to provide for the raising of money for the support of Government and for the issue of Treasury notes for the purpose of
paying the public debt, and purchasing supplies for the military
forces employed for defence in the present war, and for other
purposes, as provides for the Treasury notes therein provided
for, to bear interest from date, be rescinded and annulled :
Provided, That this ordinance shall not operate on the notes
issued before the passage of this ordinance.

2. *Be it further ordained,* That the said ordinance be so
amended as to provide and require that the whole of the Treasury notes hereafter to be issued under the provision of said
ordinance, one-half shall be issued of the denominations of five
dollars, one-fourth of the denominations of ten dollars, and the
other fourth of the denominations of twenty dollars, and in the
course of issuing the said notes, from time to time, the said relative proportions shall be observed as near as may be.

Passed and ratified in open Convention, 25th day of January,
1862.

W. N. EDWARDS,

Teste :   Pres. of Convention.

WALTER L. STEELE, Secretary,
L. C. EDWARDS, Ass't Secretary.

[No. 3.]

A RESOLUTION AUTHORIZING WM. B. GULICK TO USE CENSUS RETURNS.

Resolved, That the Secretary of State be authorized to allow Wm. B. Gulick to use, either in or out of his office, for two months, the Census Returns of 1860, or until they shall be called for by an authorized agent of the Government of the Confederate States : *Provided* the same be not removed from the City of Raleigh.

Passed and ratified in open Convention the 25th day of January, A. D., 1862.

W. N. EDWARDS,
Teste :   Pres. of Convention.
WALTER L. STEELE, Secretary,
L. C. EDWARDS, Ass't Secretary.

[No. 4.]

AN ORDINANCE TO RATIFY AND CONFIRM THE ACTS AND JUDICIAL PROCEEDINGS OF THE SUPERIOR COURTS LATELY HELD BY HIS HONOR, JUDGE FRENCH, IN THE COUNTIES OF HENDERSON, BUNCOMBE, MADISON AND YANCEY.

WHEREAS, The Superior Courts for the counties of Henderson, Buncombe, Madison and Yancey, at the Fall Terms thereof were, by mistake, held at the wrong time ; and whereas, pleas were filed, judgments rendered, recognizances entered into, judgments found, and various other acts were done by said courts :

1. *Be it ordained by the Delegates of the people of North Carolina in Convention assembled, and it is hereby ordained by the authority of the same,* That the said pleas, judgments, recognizances, indictments, and all other judicial proceedings,

which were rendered, entered and found at the terms of the courts aforesaid, are hereby made valid, and in all things ratified and confirmed.

2. *Be it further ordained,* That the Courts of Pleas and Quarter Sessions to be held hereafter for the counties of Henderson, Buncombe, Madison, Yancey and Polk, at the Fall Terms, be held at the following times, viz : Henderson, on the second Monday after the fourth Monday in September ; Buncombe, on the third Monday after the fourth Monday in September ; Madison, on the fourth Monday after the fourth Monday in September ; Yancey, on the fifth Monday after the fourth Monday in September ; and Polk on the twelfth Monday after the fourth Monday in September in each and every year. This section to continue in force until the same may be repealed by act of the Legislature or otherwise.

Passed and ratified in open Convention the 27th day of January, A. D., 1862.

W. N. EDWARDS,
Pres. of Convention.

Teste :

WALTER L. STEELE, Secretary,
L. C. EDWARDS, Ass't Secretary.

———

[No. 5.]

AN ORDINANCE TO ABROGATE THE FOURTH SECTION OF AN ACT OF THE LEGISLATURE OF THE STATE OF NORTH CAROLINA, PASSED AT THE LAST EXTRA SESSION, ENTITLED "AN ACT ENTITLED REVENUE."

Be it ordained by the Delegates of the people of North Carolina in Convention assembled, and it is hereby ordained by the authority of the same, That the fourth section of an act of the last extra session of the General Assembly of the State of

North Carolina, entitled "An Act entitled Revenue," be, and the same is hereby annulled and abrogated.

Passed and ratified in open Convention the 30th day of January, A. D., 1862.

W. N. EDWARDS,
Pres. of Convention.

Teste :
WALTER L. STEELE, Secretary,
L. C. EDWARDS, Ass't Secretary.

[No. 6.]
AN ORDINANCE TO ENCOURAGE THE MINING AND MANUFACTURING OF SALT IN THE INTERIOR OF THIS STATE.

WHEREAS, It is of great importance to manufacture Salt in the interior of this State ; and whereas, a company has been incorporated under the name and style of "The Chatham Salt Mining and Manufacturing Company," which is operating for that purpose in the county of Chatham ; therefore,

1. *Be it ordained by the Delegates of the people of North Carolina in Convention assembled, and it is hereby ordained by the authority of the same,* That the President and operatives of said company, to the number of six, be, and they are hereby exempted from militia duty, for the space of six months, except in case of invasion, insurrection, or upon a requisition for troops by the President of the Confederate States.

2. *Be it further ordained,* That said company may increase its capital stock to an amount not exceeding ten thousand dollars.

3. *Be it further ordained,* That the capital stock of said company be exempted from taxation for six months.

Passed and ratified in open Convention the 30th day of January, A. D., 1862.

W. N. EDWARDS,
Pres. of Convention.

Teste :
WALTER L. STEELE, Secretary,
L. C. EDWARDS, Ass't Secretary.

[No. 7.]

AN ORDINANCE IN ADDITION TO AND AMEND-
MENT OF AN ACT OF THE GENERAL ASSEMBLY,
RATIFIED THE 15TH DAY OF FEBRUARY, 1861.
ENTITLED "AN ACT TO INCORPORATE THE
CHATHAM RAILROAD COMPANY," AND TO RE-
PEAL AN ACT SUPPLEMENTAL THERETO, RAT-
IFIED THE 23RD DAY OF FEBRUARY, 1861.

1. *Be it ordained by the Delegates of the people of North
Carolina in Convention assembled, and it is hereby ordained by
the authority of the same,* That section first of an act of the
General Assembly, ratified the fifteenth day of February, one
thousand eight hundred and sixty-one, entitled "An Act in-
corporating the Chatham Railroad Company," be amended by
inserting after the words, "from the Coalfields, in the county
of Chatham, through said county," the words, connect with the
North Carolina Railroad at, so as to make the section read,
" to connect with the North Carolina Railroad at Raleigh, or
some point west of Raleigh not exceeding twelve miles."

2. *Be it further ordained,* That the proviso in section four
of said act of the General Assembly be stricken out.

3. *Be it further ordained,* That an act of the General Assembly, ratified on the twenty-third day of February, one
thousand eight hundred and sixty-one, entitled "An Act supplemental to an act passed at the present session of the General Assembly, entitled an act to incorporate the Chatham
Railroad Company," be, and the same is hereby repealed and
abrogated.

4. *Be it further ordained,* That all such solvent corporations as may or shall subscribe to the capital stock of the said
Chatham Railroad Company, may make their bonds payable to
the Public Treasurer of the State of North Carolina for the
amount of their subscriptions to said capital stock, and no more ;
which said bonds are to be signed by the Presidents, and under
the seals respectively of said corporations, and made for any

sums not under five hundred dollars each, to bear interest at the rate of six per cent. per annum, which interest is to be paid semi-annually, to-wit : the first Monday in January and July in each and every year ; and the principal of said bonds to be made payable twenty years after date ; and these bonds, so authorized to be made, may be deposited with the Public Treasurer of the State, who shall then issue and deliver to the several corporations so subscribing and depositing their bonds, as aforesaid, the coupon bonds of the State of North Carolina, to the amount of their subscriptions respectively, and made for the sums of five hundred dollars and one thousand dollars, to bear interest at the rate of six per cent. per annum, which interest is to be paid semi-annually, on the first Monday in January and July in each and every year, and the principal of said bonds to be made payable twenty years after date : *Provided*, That said bonds shall not exceed, in the aggregate, the sum of eight hundred thousand dollars ; and *Provided, also,* That said Chatham Railroad Company shall execute and deliver to the Governor of the State of North Carolina a deed of mortgage under the seal of said company, wherein and whereby shall be conveyed to the Governor and his successors in office, for the use and benefit of the State, all the estate, both real and personal, belonging to said company, or in any manner pertaining to the same, conditioned for indemnifying and saving harmless the State of North Carolina from the payment of the whole or any part of the bonds of the State, authorized by this ordinance to be made by the Public Treasurer, and delivered to the several corporations subscribing as aforesaid to the capital stock of said Chatham Railroad Company. In addition to the deed of mortgage, hereinbefore required to be executed and delivered by the Chatham Railroad Company, the State of North Carolina shall, by this ordinance, have a lein upon the estate, both real and personal, of said company, which they may now have or may hereafter acquire, to secure the principal and interest of the bonds of this State authorized to be issued as aforesaid.

5. *Be it further ordained,* That said bonds of the State, so made by the Public Treasurer, shall be received by the said Chatham Railroad Company in payment of subscriptions made as aforesaid by such corporations to the capital stock of said Chatham Railroad Company.

6. *Be it further ordained,* That said corporations so subscribing and depositing their bonds as aforesaid with the Treasurer of the State, shall be allowed to redeem their bonds at any time before maturity, in the currency of the State, on giving thirty days notice to the Treasurer of this State of their intention so to do.

7. *Be it further ordained,* That the said railroad may be constructed with termini at any point or points in the said Coalfields region that the stockholders in said company may agree upon with the approbation of the Board of Internal Improvements.

8. *Be it further ordained,* That the corporate authorities of incorporated towns subscribing to the capital stock of said Chatham Railroad Company, in order to provide for the payment of their subscriptions, and of the principal and interest of bonds for that purpose, by them issued, shall have authority to lay and collect taxes from all subjects, which, under the charters of said towns, are taxable.

9. *Be it further ordained,* That the solvency of such corporations as may desire to subscribe to the capital stock of said Chatham Railroad Company shall be judged of by the Board of Internal Improvements.

10. *Be it further ordained,* That all laws and parts of laws, all acts or parts of acts inconsistent with the provisions of this ordinance, are hereby repealed and abrogated.

Passed and ratified in open Convention the 30th day of January, A. D., 1862.

W. N. EDWARDS,
Pres. of Convention.

Teste :
WALTER L. STEELE, Secretary,
L. C. EDWARDS, Ass't Secretary.

[No. 8.]
AN ORDINANCE TO INCORPORATE THE PIEDMONT RAILROAD COMPANY.

1. *Be it ordained by the Delegates of the people of North Carolina in Convention assembled, and it is hereby ordained by the authority of the same,* That a company by the name and style of the "Piedmont Railroad Company," be, and the same is hereby incorporated, with a capital stock of fifteen hundred thousand dollars, divided into shares of one hundred dollars each, for the purpose of constructing a railroad on the best, cheapest, most direct and practicable route from the Richmond and Danville Railroad to the North Carolina Railroad.

2. *Be it further ordained,* That for the purpose of creating the capital stock of said company, the following persons be, and they are hereby appointed general commissioners : Wm. T. Sutherlin, of Danville ; William P. Watt, John H. Dillard, George D. Boyd and William B. Carter, of Rockingham ; Phil. Barrow, John F. Poindexter and A. J. Stafford, of Forsyth county ; William A. Lash, John J. Martin and James Riason, of Stokes county ; Jesse H. Lindsay, Levi M. Scott and Ralph Gorrell, of Guilford county ; Bedford Brown, Thomas D. Johnston, Allen Green and Montford McGee, of Caswell county ; Giles Mebane, Jesse Gant and Eli F. Watson, of Alamance ; John W. Cunningham, Edwin G. Read and Thos. McGee, of the county of Person ; William Johnston, of the town of Charlotte ; James C. Turrentine and Wm. F. Strayhorn, of the county of Orange ; Benjamin A. Kittrell, of the town of Lexington ; H. C. Jones, Sr., of Salisbury ; Jonathan Worth, of the town of Ashboro' ; Wm. P. Taylor, of Pittsboro' ; whose duty it shall be to direct the opening of books for subscriptions of stock at such times and places, and under such persons as they, or a majority of them, may deem proper, and in the mean time it shall and may be lawful for books of subscriptions to said stock may be opened in the town of Charlotte under the direction of John A. Young, Wm. Johnston and

2

James W. Osborne, or any one of them; in Concord, under the direction of V. M. Barringer, Caleb Phifer and Daniel Coleman, or any one of them; in Salisbury, under the direction of Nathaniel Boyden, N. N. Fleming, J. I. Shaver, or any one of them; at Lexington, under the direction of Wm. R. Holt, John P. Mabrey and Samuel Hargrove, or any one of them; at High Point, under the direction of W. F. Bowman, Dr. Robert Lindsay and Nathan Hunt, or any one of them; at Greensboro', under the direction of James Sloan, Jed. II. Lindsay and J. A. Long, or any one of them; at Salem, under the direction of D. H. Starbuck, J. G. Lash, Francis Fries and C. L. Bonner, or any one of them; at Danbury, under the direction of Nathaniel Moody, A. H. Joyce and S. Taylor, or any one of them; at Graham, under the direction of Thos. Ruffin, Jr., John Trollinger and Edward Holt, or any one of them; at Roxboro', under the direction of Chas. Winstead, Dr. C. H. Jordan and Green Williams, or any one of them; at Yanceyville, under the direcfion of John Kerr, Dr. N. M. Roan and Thomas W. Graves, or any one of them; at Milton, under the direction of Samuel Watkins, John Wilson and Thomas Donaho, or any one of them; at Wentworth, under the direction of John W. Ellington, W. M. Ellington and B. J. Low, or any one of them; at Madison, under the direction of Wm. L. Scales, Joseph H. Cardwell and Nicholas Dalton, or any one of them; at Leaksville, under the direction of Geo. L. Aiken, Jones W. Burton and E. T. Brodnax, or any one of them; at High Rock, under the direction of Francis L. Simpson, Dr. R. H. Scales and George W. Garret, or any one of them; at Danville, Va., under the direction of William T. Sutherlin, James M. Williams and Dr. T. P. Atkinson, or any one of them; at Hillsboro', under the direction of J. C. Turrentine, Henry K. Nash and W. F. Strayhorn, or any one of them; and in the city of Richmond, Va., under the direction of A. Y. Stokes, Lewis E. Harvey and Thomas N. Brockenbrough, or any one of them; and said commissioners shall have power to appoint a Chairman of their body, Treasurer, and all other officers their organization may require, and sue for and recover all sums of money that ought, under this ordinance, to be recovered by them in the name of said corporation.

3. *Be it further ordained,* That all persons who are, by this ordinance authorized, or who may be hereafter, by the general coommissioners, authorized to open books of subscription, may do so at any time after the passage of this ordinance, upon giving twenty days notice of the time and place when said books shall be opened, and said books shall be kept open for the space of thirty days, at least, and as long thereafter as the general commissioners shall direct ; and that all subscriptions of stock shall be in shares of one hundred dollars, the subscriber paying, at the time he makes his subscription, five dollars on each share by him subscribed, to the person or persons authorized to receive such subscriptions ; and upon closing the books, all such sums as shall have thus been received of subscribers, on the first cash instalment, shall be paid over to the general commissioners, by the persons receiving the same, and in case of failure to pay, as aforesaid, such person or persons, receiving said money, shall be personally liable to said general commissioners, before the organization of said company, and to the company itself, after the organization, to be recovered within the Superior Courts of Law within this State, in the county where such delinquent resides, or if he resides in another State, then, in any court in such State having competent jurisdiction. The general commissioners shall have power to call on and require all persons empowered to receive subscriptions of stock, at any time, and from time to time, as a majority of them may think' proper, to make return of the stock by them respectively received, and to make payment of all sums of money paid by subscribers ; that all persons receiving subscriptions of stock shall pass a receipt to the subscriber or subscribers for the payment of the first instalment, as heretofore required to be paid, and upon their settlement with the general commissioners as aforesaid, it shall be, the duty of said general commissioners, in like manner, to pass their receipts for all

sums thus received to the persons from whom received, and such receipts shall be taken and held to be good and sufficient vouchers to persons holding them; that subscriptions of stock may be received as aforesaid or as hereafter provided for, to the amount of fifteen hundred thousand dollars.

4. *Be it further ordained,* That it shall be the duty of said general commissioners to direct and authorize said books of subscription to be kept open until the sum of one hundred thousand dollars, at least, shall be subscribed in the manner aforesaid, and as soon as the said sum of one hundred thousand dollars, or upwards, shall be subscribed in manner aforesaid, and the sum of five dollars on each share paid as aforesaid, the subscribers to said stock shall be, and they are hereby declared to be a body politic, and corporate in fact and in law, by the name and style of the " Piedmont Railroad Company," with all the corporate powers and authority thereby created and granted, to be held and exercised by said company and their successors and assigns, in perpetuity, and by that name shall be capable, in law and in equity, to purchase, hold, lease, rent, sell or convey estates, real and personal, and to acquire the same by gift, devise or otherwise, so far as shall be necessary for the purposes embraced within the scope, object and intent of this charter, and shall have perpetual succession and a common seal, which may use, alter or renew at pleasure, and by their corporate name, may sue and be sued, plead and be impleaded, in any court of law in this State or any other State ; and shall have, possess and enjoy, all rights, privileges and immunities which railroad corporate bodies may and of right do exercise, and may make such by-laws, rules and regulations as are necessary for the government of the corporation, or for effecting the object for which it is created, not inconsistent with the laws of this State or of the Confederate States of America.

5. *Be it further ordained,* That as soon as the sum of one hundred thousand dollars or upwards shall be subscribed, as aforesaid, it shall be the duty of the general commissioners to appoint a time for the stockholders to meet in the town of

Greensboro, in the county of Guilford, which they shall cause to be previously published for the space of thirty days, in one or more newspapers; at which time and place, the said stockholders shall, in person or by proxy, proceed to elect by ballot nine directors of the company, and to enact all such regulations and by-laws as may be necessary for the government of said corporation, and the transaction of its business. The persons elected directors at this meeting shall serve such period not exceeding one year as the stockholders may direct; and at this meeting, the stockholders shall fix on the day and place or places when and where the subsequent election of directors shall be held, and such elections shall thenceforth be annually made; but if the day of annual elections should pass without any election of directors, the corporation shall not thereby be dissolved; but the directors in office shall so remain until others are appointed, and it shall be lawful on any other day to make and hold such elections in such manner as may be prescribed by a by-law of the corporation.

6. *Be it further ordained,* That the affairs of said company shall be managed by a general board, to consist of nine directiors, to be elected by the stockholders from among themselves, at their first and subsequent general annual meetings, and no stockholder shall be elected a director, nor serve as such, unless he be at the time of his election the owner of five shares of stock, and shall continue to hold the same during the term of his service as director.

7. *Be it further ordained,* That the President of said company shall be chosen by ballot by a majority of the Directors from among themselves, with a salary to be fixed by the stockholders in general meeting.

8. *Be it further ordained,* That all stockholders, not being aliens, shall be entitled to vote either in person or by proxy. the proxy being a stockholder, at all general meetings, and the vote to which each stockholder shall be entitled, shall be according to the number of shares he may hold as hereinafter provided.

9. *Be it further ordained,* That at the first general meeting of the stockholders, under this ordinance, a majority of all the shares subscribed shall be represented before proceeding to business ; and if a sufficient number do not appear on the day appointed, those who do attend shall have power to adjourn from time to time until a regular meeting be thus formed, and at such meeting the stockholders may provide by a by-law as to the number of stockholders, and the amount of stock to be held by them, which shall constitute a quorum for the transaction of business at all subsequent meetings.

10. *Be it further ordained,* That the general commissioners shall make their return of shares of stock subscribed for, at the first general meeting of the stockholders, and pay over to the directors elected at that meeting, or their authorized agent, all sums of money received from subscribers ; and on failure to do so, they shall be personally liable to said company, to be recovered in like manner as other debts due the company.

11. *Be it further ordained,* That the Board of Directors may fill all vacancies which may occur in it during the period for which they have been elected, and in the absence of the President, may fill his place by electing a President *pro tem.* from among their number.

12. *Be it further ordained,* That' said Board of Directors shall have power and authority to open books for further subscriptions to the stock of said company at such times and under such persons as they may designate, in the event the whole stock be not subscribed before the first general meeting of the stockholders, and to open and keep open such books, from time to time, until the whole amount of capital stock be subscribed.

13. *Be it further ordained,* That said company shall have power and proceed to construct, as speedily as possible, a Railroad with one or more tracks, from the North Carolina Railroad to the Richmond and Danville Railroad in Virginia, to be used and operated by steam power, and to the end that the said corporated may have power and authority to construct said road within the limits of the State of Virginia—this charter

shall be transmitted by the President of this Convention to the Governor of Virginia, to the end that the legislative sanction of that State, approving the ordinance, may be given to said company, to construct the railroad as aforesaid within the limits of that State: *Provided*, That the company formed under this charter shall have no power to discriminate, on either freight or travel, against the North Carolina Railroad, or roads in North Carolina connected with it.

14. *Be it further ordained*, That said company shall have the exclusive right of conveyance or transportation of persons, goods, merchandise, and produce, over the road constructed by them, at such charges as may be fixed upon by a majority of the directors; and the said company may farm out their rights of transportation over their said railroad, subject to the rules above mentioned; and said company, and every person who may have received from them the right of transportation of goods, wares, and produce on said road, shall be deemed and and taken to be a commmon carrier, as respects everything entrusted to them or him for transportation.

15. *Be it further ordained*, That the Board of Directors may call for the payment of the sums subscribed as stock in said company in such instalments as the interest of the said company may require; the call for each payment shall be published in one or more papers in this State for two months before the day of payment, and on failure of any stockholder to pay each instalment as thus required, the directors may sell at public auction, on a previous notice of ten days, for cash, all the stock subscribed for in said company by such stockholders, and convey the same to the purchaser at said sale, discharged from further liabilities; and if said sale of stock does not produce a sum sufficient to pay off the incidental expenses of sale, and the entire amount owing by such stockholder to the company for such subscription of stock, then and in that case the whole of such balance shall be held and taken as due at once to the company, and may be recovered of such stockholder or his executors, administrators or assigns, at suit of said·company

either by summary motion in any court of supreme jurisdiction
in the county where the delinquent resides, on a previous notice
of ten days to said subscribers, or by action of assumpit in
any court of competent jurisdiction, or by warrant before a
Justice of the Peace when the sum does not exceed one hundred dollars ; and in all cases of assignment of stock before
the whole amount has been paid to the company, then, for all
sums due on such stock, both the original subscribers and the
first and all the subsequent assignees shall be held liable to the
company, and the same may be recovered as above described.

16. *Be it further ordained*, That said company shall issue
certificates of stock to its members, and said stock may be
transferred in such manner and form as may be directed by the
by-laws of the company.

17. *Be it further ordained*, That the debt of the stockholders due to the company for stock therein, either original
proprietor, or as first or subsequent assignee, shall be considered
with equal dignity with judgments in the distribution of the
assets of a deceased stockholder by his legal representatives.

18. *Be it further ordained*, That the Board of Directors
shall, once a year, at least, make a full report on the state of
the company and its affairs, to a general meeting of the stockholders, and oftener if required by a by-law, and shall have
power to call a general meeting of the stockholders when the
board may deem expedient; and the company may provide in
their by-laws for occasional meetings being called, and prescribe the mode thereof.

19. *Be it further ordained*, That the said company may purchase, have and hold, in fee or for a term of years, any lands,
tenements, or hereditaments which may be necessary for said
road, or appurtenances thereof, or for the erection of depositories, store houses, houses for the officers, servants, or agents of
the company, or for the workshops or foundries to be used for
said company, or for procuring stone or other materials necessary to the construction of the road, or for effecting transportation thereon.

20. *Be it further ordained,* That tho company shall have the right, when necessary, to conduct the said road across or along any public road or water course : *Provided,* That the said company shall not obstruct any public road without constructing another equally as good and convenient.

21. *Be it further ordained,* That when any land or right of way may be required by said company for the purpose of constructing their road, and for want of agreement as to the value thereof, or for any other cause, the same can not be purchased from the owner or owners—the same many be taken at a valuation to be made by five freeholders, selected by the County Court in the county where the right of way is situated : *Provided, nevertheless,* That if any person or persons over whose lands the road may pass, or if said company should be dissatisfied with the valuation of said freeholders, then, and in that case, the party so dissatisfied may have an appeal to the Superior Court in the county where the damage is done, or in either county where the land may lie, under the same rules, regulations and restrictions as in other classes of appeal ; the proceeding of the said freeholders, accompanied with a full description of said land or right of way, shall be returned under the hands and seals of a majority of them to the court from which the order was made, there to remain a matter of record ; and the lands or right of way so valued, shall vest in the said company so long as the same may be used for purposes of said railroad, as soon as the valuation shall have been made, or when refused, may have been tendered : *Provided,* That on application for the appointment of freeholders under this section, it shall be made to appear to the satisfaction of the court, that at least ten days' previous notice has been given by the applicant to the owner or owners of the land proposed to be condemned, or if the owner or owners be infants or *non compos mentis,* then to the guardian or guardians of such owner or owners, if such guardian can be found within the county, or if he cannot be found, then such appointment shall not be made unless notice of the application shall have been published at least one month

3

next preceding in some newspaper printed as conveniently as may be to the court house of the county, and shall have been posted at the door of the court house on the first day of the term of said court to which the application is made : *Provided, further,* That the valuation provided for in this section shall be made on oath by the freeholders aforesaid, which oath, any Justice of the Peace, or clerk, is authorized to administer : *Provided, further,* That the right of condemnation herein granted, shall not authorize the said company to invade the dwelling house, yard, garden or burial ground of any individual without his consent.

22. *Be it further ordained,* That the right of said company to condemn lands in the manner as aforesaid, shall extend to the condemning one hundred feet on each side of the track of the road, measuring from the centre of the same, unless in case of deep cuts and fillings, when said company shall have power to condemn as much in addition thereto as may be necessary for the purpose of constructing said road, and the company shall also have power to condemn and appropriate lands in like manner for the constructing and building of depots, shops, warehouses, buildings for servants, agents, and persons employed on the road, not exceeding four acres to any one lot or station.

23. *Be it further ordained,* That in the absence of any contract or contracts with said company in relation to the lands through which the said road may pass, signed by the owner thereof, or his agent or any claimant or person in possession thereof, it shall be presumed that the land upon which the said road may be constructed, together with the space of one hundred feet on each side of the centre of said road, has been granted to the said company by the owner thereof, and the said said company shall have good right and title thereto, and shall have, hold and enjoy the same as long as the same be used for the purposes of the road, and no longer, unless the person or persons owning the said land at the time that part of the said road which may be on the said land was finished, or those claiming under him, her or them, shall apply for an assignment of the

value of said lands as hereinbefore directed, within two years next after that part of the said road which may be on said lands was finished, and in case the said owner, or those claiming under him, her or them, shall not apply within two years next after the said part was finished, he, she or they shall be forever barred from recovering said land, or having any assessment or compensation therefor : *Provided*, Nothing herein contained shall affect the rights of *feme coverts*, or infants, until two years after the removal of their respective disabilities.

24. *Be it further ordained*, That all lands not heretofore granted to any person within one hundred feet of the centre of said road, shall vest in the company so soon as the line of the road is definitely laid out through it, and any grant of said land shall thereafter be void.

25. *Be it further ordained*, That if any person or persons shall intrude upon said railroad, by any manner of use thereof, or of the right and privilege connected therewith, without the permission, or contrary to the will of said company, he, she or they may be indicted for a misdemeanor, and upon conviction, fined and imprisoned by any court of competent jurisdiction.

26. *Be it further ordained*, That if any person or persons shall willfully and maliciously destroy, or in any manner hurt or damage, or shall willfully and maliciously cause, or aid or assist, or counsel and advise any other person or persons to destroy, or in any manner to hurt, damage, injure or obstruct the said railroad, or any bridge or vehicle used for or in the transportation thereon, any water-tank, warehouse, or other property of said company, such person or persons, so offending, shall be liable to be indicted therefor, and on conviction, shall be imprisoned not less than one nor more than six months, and pay a fine, not exceeding five hundred dollars, nor less than twenty dollars, at the discretion of the court before which said conviction shall take place, and shall be further liable to pay all expenses for repairing the same ; and it shall not be competent for any one so offending against the provisions of this clause to defend himself by pleading or giving in evidence that he was

the owner, agent, or servant of the owner of the land where
such destruction, hurt, damage, injury or obstruction was done
at the time the same was done or caused to be done.

27. *Be it further ordained*, That every obstruction to the
safe and free passage of vehicles on said road shall be deemed
a public nuisance, and be abated as such by any officer, agent or
servant of said company, and the person causing such obstruction may be indicted for erecting a public nuisance.

28. *Be it further ordained*, That the said company shall
have the right to take, at the storehouses they may establish,
or annex to their railroad, all goods, wares, merchandise, and
produce intended for transportation, to prescribe the rules of
priority, and charge and receive such just and reasonable compensation for storage as they, by rules, may establish (which
they shall cause to be published) as may be fixed, by agreement,
with the owners, which may be distinct from rates of transportation : *Provided*, That the said company shall not charge nor
receive storage on goods, wares, merchandise or produce which
may be delivered to them at their regular depositories for imme-
diate transportation, and which the company may have the
power to transport immediately.

29. *Be it further ordained*, That the profits of the company,
or so much thereof as the General Board may deem advisable,
shall, when the affairs of the company will permit, be semi-
annually divided among the stockholders in proportion to the
stock each may own.

30. *Be it further ordained*, That the following officers and
servants and persons in the actual employment of said company
be, and they are hereby exempt from the performance of jury
and ordinary militia duty : The President and Treasurer, the
Board of Directors, Chief and Assistant Engineers, the Secretary
and Accountant of the company, keepers of the depositories,
guards stationed on the road and at the bridges, and such persons as may be working the locomotive engines and traveling
with the cars for the purpose of attending to the transport of
produce, goods and passengers on the road.

31. *Be it further ordained,* That if the Legislature of Virginia shall sanction this charter, and authorize the construction of said road within the limits of Virginia to the Richmond and Danville Railroad, and said road shall be so constructed, the said corporation hereby created shall, nevertheless, have power and authority to construct and build one or more branches of said road to the Coalfields of Dan River, and the navigable waters on Smith's River, in the county of Rockingham, and are hereby vested with the rights, powers, privileges and immunities to build and construct said branch or branches with which they are invested to build the main road ; and the said road, with its branches, authorized to be constructed under this charter, shall be of the same guage as the North Carolina Railroad ; and the North Carolina Railroad Company shall have the right, under this charter, to construct a branch of their road from Hillsboro' at or near Danville.

32. *Be it further ordained,* That for the purpose of ascertaining the best route for said road and its branches, and to locate the same, it shall be lawful for said company, by its engineers, servants and agents, to enter upon, examine and survey any land or lands that they may wish to examine for such purpose, free from any liability whatever.

33. *Be it further ordained,* That any one or more of the solvent incorporate railroad companies of the said States, and also the Confederate States of America, may subscribe for stock in said company, and should the Confederate States of America subscribe for and take the whole of such stock, or the larger part thereof, power and authority are given to said Confederate States of America to appoint for the time being the whole of the said Directors, anything in this ordinance to the contrary notwithstanding, and at once locate and commence the construction of said road, and hold the stock so taken by them until individuals and corporations shall be prepared to receive an assignment of the same, or any part or parts thereof, as hereinafter provided.

34. *Be it further ordained*, That as soon as, under the supervision of the general commissioners, as by this ordinance provided, there shall be subscribed by the Confederate States of America, incorporated companies, or solvent individuals, not less than one hundred thousand dollars of stock, with the five per cent. thereon paid in, the same shall be certified by said general commissioners to said Directors, on which being done, it shall be the duty of said Directors to have the names of such stockholders recorded on the books of said company, together with the stock subscribed by each, and to cause to have issued to said stockholders certificates of stock in said company, (to each in proportion to the subscriptions made by them,) when they shall have paid up their subscriptions in full, including in their payments the five per cent. which they shall have paid to the said general commissioners, and which the said general commissioners, as hereinbefore provided, shall pay to said company.

35. *Be it further ordained*, That as soon as subscribers other than the Confederate States of America, as herein provided, shall have their names as stockholders recorded on the books of said company as owners of not less than one hundred thousand dollars of stock, with the five per cent. thereon paid in, from and after that time such stockholders, in all general meetings, shall have power to elect five of the said nine Directors, and the President of the Confederate States of America, or such other person as the Confederate States may determine, to appoint four of said Directors, and continue to do so until the stock of the said Confederate States, by sale or transfer, shall be reduced to less than half of the entire stock of said company ; then, and from and after that time, the vote of the said Confederate States of America in the election of Directors, and on all other questions, shall be in proportion to the stock held by them : *Provided*, That at such elections no stockholder shall give more than two hundred votes.

. 36. *Be it further ordained*, That full right and privilege is hereby reserved to the State, or to any company hereafter to be incorporated under the authority of this State, to connect with the road hereby provided for, any other railroad leading therefrom to any part or parts of this State: *Provided*, That in joining such connection, no injury shall be done to the works of the company hereby incorporated.

37. *Be it further ordained*, That the corporate franchises and privileges hereby granted shall cease and determine at the expiration of ninety-nine years from the day of the passage of this ordinance.

Passed and ratified in open Convention the 8th day of February, A. D., 1862.

W. N. EDWARDS,
Teste: Pres. of Convention.
WALTER L. STEELE, Secretary,
L. C. EDWARDS, Ass't Secretary.

[No. 9.]

AN ORDINANCE TO INCORPORATE THE WASHINGTON AND TARBORO' RAILROAD COMPANY.

1. *Be it ordained by the Delegates of the people of North Carolina in Convention assembled, and it is hereby ordained by the authority of the same*, That for the purpose of effecting a railroad communication between the town of Washington and the town of Tarboro', the formation of a corporate company, with the capital of four hundred thousand dollars, is hereby authorized, to be called the Washington and Tarboro' Railroad Company, and when formed in compliance with the conditions hereinafter prescribed, to have a corporate existence as a body politic in perpetuity.

2. *Be it further ordained*, That the said company be, and the same is hereby authorized to construct a railroad from the town of Washington, in the county of Beaufort, through the counties of Pitt and Edgecombe, to the town of Tarboro'.

3. *Be it further ordained*, That for the purpose of raising
the capital stock of said company, it shall be lawful to open
books under the direction of the following named Commissioners, to-wit : At Washington, under the direction of John Myers,
Joseph Potts, Benjamin F. Havens, B. M. Selby, and George
H. Brown ; at Pactolus, under the direction of Churchill Per-
kins, Peyton A. Atkinson, J. G. B. Grimes, Rippon Ward, and
Henry Stancill ; at Tarboro', under the direction of John S.
Dancy, R. H. Pender, Robert R. Bridgers, William S. Battle,
and James R. Thigpen, and at such other places and under
the direction of such other persons as a majority of the com-
missoners first named may deem proper, for the purpose of receiving subscriptions to the amount of four hundred thousand
dollars, in shares of fifty dollars each.

4. *Be it further ordained*, That the commissioners above
named, and all other persons who may hereafter be authorized
as aforesaid to open books for subscriptions, shall open the same
at any time after the ratification of this ordinance, first giving
ten days' notice thereof, of the time and place, in one or more of
the newspapers published in Washington and Tarboro' ; and
the said books, when opened, shall be kept open for the space
of thirty days, at least, and as long thereafter as the commissioners first above named shall direct, and the said first commissioners shall have power to call on and require all persons
empowered to receive subscriptions of stock, at any time, and
from time to time, as a majority of them may think proper, to
make return of subscriptions of stock by them respectively received.

5. *Be it further ordained*, That whenever the sum of ten
thousand dollars shall be subscribed in the manner and form
aforesaid, the subscribers, their executors, administrators or
assigns, shall be, and they are hereby declared incorporated
into a company by the name and style of the Washington and
Tarboro' Railroad Company, and by that name shall be capable in law and equity of purchasing, holding, selling, leasing,
and conveying estates, real, personal and mixed, and acquiring

the same by gift or devise, so far as shall be necessary for the purposes embraced within the scope, object and intent of their charter, and no further; and shall have perpetual succession, and by their corporate name may sue and be sued, plead and be impleaded in any court of law and equity in this State, and may have and use a common seal, which they may alter and renew at pleasure, and shall have and enjoy all other rights and immunities which other railroad corporate bodies may, and of right do exercise, and make all by-laws, rules, and regulations that are necessary for the government of the corporation, or effecting the object for which it was created, not inconsistent with the Constitution and laws of the State.

6. *Be it further ordained,* That it shall be the duty of the commissioners named in this ordinance for receiving subscriptions in Washington, or a majority of them, as soon as the sum of ten thousand dollars shall have been subscribed, in manner aforesaid, to give public notice thereof, and at the same time to call a general meeting of the stockholders, giving at least fifteen days' notice of the time and place of meeting; a majority of the stockholders being represented in person, or by proxy, shall proceed to elect a President and Treasurer, and six Directors, out of the number of stockholders; and the said Directors shall have power to perform all the duties necessary in the government of the corporation, and the transaction of its business; and the persons elected as aforesaid, shall serve such period, not exceeding one year, as the stockholders may direct: and, at that meeting, the stockholders shall fix on the day and place or places where the subsequent election of President, Treasurer and Directors shall be held, and such election shall, thenceforth, be annually made; but if the day of the annual election of officers should, under any circumstances, pass without an election, the corporation shall not thereby be dissolved, but the officers formerly elected shall continue in office until a new election takes place.

7. *Be it further ordained,* That the election of officers aforesaid, shall be, by ballot, each stockholder having as many votes

as he has shares in the stock of the company, and the person having the greatest number of votes polled, shall be considered duly elected to the office for which he is nominated, and at all elections and upon all votes taken at any meeting of the stockholders, upon any by-law or any of the affairs of the company, each share of the stock shall be entitled to one vote, to be represented either in person or by proxy; and proxies may be verified in such manner as the by-laws of the company may prescribe.

8. *Be it further ordained*, That the Board of Directors may fill any vacancies that may occur in it during the period for which they have been elected, and in the absence of the President, may appoint a President, *pro tempore*, to fill his place.

9. *Be it further ordained*, That the Board of Directors may call for the sums subscribed as stock in said company in such instalments as the interest of said company may, in their opinion, require. The call for each payment shall be published in one or more newspapers of the State, for one month before the day of payment, and on failure of any stockholder to pay each instalment as thus required, the Directors may sell, at public auction, on a previous notice of ten days, for cash, all the stock subscribed for in said company by such stockholder, and convey the same to the purchaser at the said sale, and if the said sale of stock does not produce a sum sufficient to pay off the incidental expenses of the sale, and the entire amount owing by such stockholder to the company for such subscription of stock, then, and in that case, the whole of such balance shall be held as due at once to the company, and may be recovered of such stockholder, or his executors, administrators or assigns, at the suit of said company, either by summary motion in any court of superior jurisdiction in the county where the delinquent resides, on previous notice of ten days to said subscriber, or by action of assumpsit, in any court of competent jurisdiction, or by warrant before a Justice of the Peace, when the sum does not exceed one hundred dollars; and in all cases of assignment of stock before the whole amount has been paid to the com-

pany, then, for all sums on such stocks, both the original subscriber and all subsequent assignees, shall be liable to the
company, and the same may be recovered as above described.

10. *Be it further ordained,* That the debt of the stockholders due to the company for stock therein, either as original
proprietor, or first or subsequent assignee, shall be considered
as of equal dignity with judgments in the distribution of assets
of a deceased stockholder by his legal representatives.

11. *Be it further ordained,* That said company shall issue
certificates of stock to its members, and said stock may be
transferred in such manner and form as may be directed by the
by-laws of the company.

12. *Be it further ordained,* That the said company may, at
any time, increase its capital stock to a sum sufficient to complete said road, not exceeding the additional sum of one hundred thousand dollars, by opening books of subscription of
new stock, or borrowing money on the credit of the company,
and the mortgage of its charter and works, and the manner in
which the same shall be done, in either case, shall be prescribed by the stockholders.

13. *Be it further ordained,* That all contracts or agree-
ments, authenticated by the President and Secretary of the
Board, shall be binding on the company, with or without a seal ;
such a mode of authentication shall be used as the company,
by their by-laws, may adopt.

14. *Be it further ordained,* That the said company may
purchase, in fee, or for a term of years, any lands, tenements
or hereditaments, which may be necessary for said road, or for
the erection of depositories, storehouses, houses for the officers,
servants or agents of the company, or for workshops or foundries, to be used by the company, or for procuring stone or other
material necessary to the construction of the road or effecting
transportation, and for no other purposes whatever.

15. *Be it further ordained,* That the company shall have
the right, when necessary, to construct the said railroad across
any public road or along the side of any public road : *Pro-*

vided, That the said company shall not obstruct any public road without constructing one equally as good and as convenient as the one taken by the company.

16. *Be it further ordained,* That when any lands or right of way may be required by the company for the purpose of constructing their road, building warehouses, water-stations, workshops or depositories, and for want of agreement as to the value thereof, or from any other cause, the same cannot be purchased from the owner or owners, the same may be taken at a valuation to be made by a jury of good and lawful men, to be summoned by the Sheriff of the county in which the land required by the company may lie ; and in making the said valuation, the said jury shall take into consideration the loss or damage which may occur to the owner or owners in consequence of the land or right of way being surrendered, and the benefit or advantage he, she or they may receive from the erection of said road, and shall state particularly the value and amount of each ; and the excess of loss or damage over and above the advantage and benefit shall form the measure of valuation of the land or right of way: *Provided, nevertheless,* That if any person or persons over whose lands said roads may pass, or the company should be dissatisfied with the valuation thus made, then, and in that case, either party may have an appeal to the next court of the county, to be held thereafter ; and the Sheriff shall return to said court the verdict of jury, with all the proceedings thereon, and the lands or right of way so valued by the jury shall vest in the company so long as the same may be used for the purposes of said railroad, so soon as the valuation be paid, or if refused, paid over to the clerk of the County Court: *Provided, further,* That the right of condemnation shall not authorize the said company to invade the dwelling house, yard, garden or grave-yard of any individual without. his consent.

17. *Be it further ordained,* That the right of said company to condemn land in the manner described in the above section, shall extend to the condemnation only of one hundred feet on

each side of the main track of the road, and from the cen tr of the same, except in case of deep cuts and fillings, when the said company shall have power to condemn as much in addition thereto as may be necessary for the purpose of constructing said road, and the company, in like manner, shall have power to condemn and appropriate land for the building of depots and shops, not exceeding five acres in any one lot or station.

18. *Be it further ordained*, That the said company shall have the exclusive right of conveyance or transportation of persons, goods, merchandise and produce over said road, at such charges as may be fixed by a majority of the directors.

19. *Be it further ordained*, That the profits of the company, or so much thereof as the Board of Directors may deem advisable, shall, when the affairs of the company will permit, be annually or semi-annually divided among the stockholders in proportion to the stock each may own.

20. *Be it further ordained*, That notice of process upon the President, or any of the directors thereof, shall be deemed and taken to be due and lawful notice of service upon the company.

21. *Be it further ordained*, That the company shall have power to construct branches of said road to connect with any other road that may be constructed east of the Wilmington and Weldon Railroad, and any contract that may be entered into with any other railroad company by the President and Directors of said company, after the consent of a majority of the stockholders first obtained, shall be binding on the company.

22. *Be it further ordained*, That it may be lawful for the Washington and Tarboro' Railroad Company to make and issue bonds to an amount not exceeding fifty thousand dollars, to be signed by the President of said company, under the common seal of the same, in sums of five hundred dollars each, bearing interest at the rate of seven per cent. or less per annum, to be paid semi-annually.

23. *Be it further ordained*, That to secure the faithful payment of said bonds, it may and shall be lawful for the President and Directors of the Washington and Tarboro' Railroad

Company to make, execute and deliver to such person as the company may select or appoint, a deed of trust or mortgage, under the common seal of said company, wherein shall be conveyed to the person thus appointed trustee, the road, property, income and franchise of said company, acquired or to be acquired, conditioned for the payment of the interest and final redemption of said bonds.

24. *Be it further ordained,* That all officers of the company, and servants, and persons in the actual employment of the company, may be, and they are hereby exempt from performing ordinary military duty, (except in case of insurrection or invasion,) working on public roads and serving as jurors.

25. *Be it further ordained,* That all the work hereby required, shall be executed with due diligence, and if it be not commenced within four years after the ratification of this ordinance, then this charter shall be void.

26. *Be it further ordained,* That this ordinance shall be in force from and after its ratification, and shall be regarded as a public ordinance.

Passed and ratified in open Convention the 7th February, 1862.

W. N. EDWARDS,
Pres. of Convention.

Teste :

WALTER L. STEELE, Secretary,
L. C. EDWARDS, Ass't Secretary.

[No. 10.]

AN ORDINANCE TO AUTHORIZE THE TREASURER
TO ISSUE TREASURY NOTES.

Be it ordained by the Delegates of the people of North Carolina in Convention assembled, and it is hereby ordained by the authority of the same, That the Public Treasurer be, and he is hereby authorized to issue any amount of Treasury notes, now on hand, not exceeding one hundred and twenty thousand dollars, above the denomination of twenty dollars: *Provided*, Said notes shall bear no interest: *And provided, further*, That this amount shall be a part of the three millions heretofore ordered to be isssued.

Passed and ratified in open Convention, the 4th day of February, A. D., 1862.

W. N. EDWARDS,
Teste: Pres. of Convention.
WALTER L. STEELE, Secretary,
L. C. EDWARDS, Assistant Secretary.

———

[No. 11.]
A RESOLUTION IN RELATION TO THE MINTS.

Resolved, That in the opinion of this Convention, it is of the highest importance to the interests of the Confederate States, that the Mints situated within their limits should be placed in operation at the earliest practicable period, and that the Senators and Representatives in Congress be requested to use their best exertions to obtain this object.

Passed and ratified in open Convention the 7th day of February, 1862.

W. N. EDWARDS,
Teste: Pres. of Convention.
WALTER L. STEELE, Secretary,
L. C. EDWARDS, Assistant Secretary.

———

[No. 12.]
RESOLUTION RESPECTING THE PAY OF THE THIRTY-EIGHTH REGIMENT OF NORTH CAROLINA VOLUNTEERS.

Resolved, That the pay rolls of the companies of the thirty-eighth regiment of North Carolina Volunteers be made out and received from the date of the acceptances of the companies respectively.

Passed and ratified in open Convention the 8th day of February, A. D., 1862.

W. N. EDWARDS,
Pres. of Convention.

Teste :
WALTER L. STEELE, Secretary,
L. C. EDWARDS, Ass't Secretary.

———

[No. 13.]
AN ORDINANCE CONCERNING THE LEVYING OF TAXES BY THE COUNTY COURTS.

1. *Be it ordained by the Delegates of the people of North Carolina in Convention assembled, and it is hereby ordained by the authority of the same,* That the Chairman of the County Court, and where there is no Chairman, the County Court Clerk of each and every county in this State, shall, by public notice, convene the Justices of the County Courts at their respective court houses on the first Monday in May, 1862; and a majority of the Justices being present, they shall proceed to levy taxes for county purposes, and may, in their discretion, as now provided by law, levy the taxes for school purposes; and the Clerk of the respective County Courts, shall, in such cases, enter the proceedings of said Justices on the minute docket of said County Courts, as a part of the record of said courts thus convened in special session : *Provided,* That in counties holding regular terms of their County Courts in said month of May, or the first Monday of June, the levy hereby required shall be made at such regular term.

2. *Be it further ordained,* That the act of the last extra session of the General Assembly, entitled "An Act to enlarge the powers of the County Courts for raising revenue for county purposes ;" which requires the Justices of the several County

Courts, at their first court after the first day of January in every year, to levy a tax for county and school purposes, &c., be, and the same is hereby modified and repealed, so far as the same may apply to the present year, 1862.

3. *Be it further ordained,* That this ordinance shall expire and be inapplicable after the year 1862.

4. *Be it further ordained,* That those counties in which their County Courts have already levied taxes for county and school purposes, and in those counties in which they may hereafter levy the same in ignorance of the provisions of this ordinance, the same shall be void and of no effect.

Passed and ratified in open Convention the 10th day of February, A. D., 1862.

W. N. EDWARDS,
Pres. of Convention.

Teste :

WALTER L. STEELE, Secretary,
L. C. EDWARDS, Assistant Secretary.

[No. 14.]

A RESOLUTION TO PRINT AN ORDINANCE.

Resolved by the Delegates of the people of North Carolina in Convention assembled, and it is hereby ordained by the authority of the same, That the Secretary of the State be authorized and directed to have printed three hundred copies of the ordinance this day passed, entitled " an ordinance concerning the levying of taxes by the County Courts,'' and forward one copy each to the Sheriff, County Court Clerk and Chairman of the County Court of each and every county in the State.

Passed and ratified in open Convention the 10th day of February, A. D., 1862.

W. N. EDWARDS,
Pres. of Convention.

Teste :

WALTER L. STEELE, Secretary,
L. C. EDWARDS, Ass't Secretary.

[No. 15.]

AN ORDINANCE TO AUTHORIZE THE HOLDING OF A COURT OF OYER AND TERMINER, AT WAYNESVILLE, IN HAYWOOD COUNTY.

1. *Be it ordained by the delegates of the people of North Carolina, in Convention assembled, and it is hereby ordained by the authority of the same,* That His Excellency, the Governor of the State, be, and he is hereby authorized and requested to issue a commission to any one of the Superior Court Judges of this State, to hold a court of *Oyer* and *Terminer*, at Waynesville, in the county of Haywood, for the purpose of trying the persons now in jail at that place, charged with high crimes, which Judge, when so commissioned, shall be clothed with all the powers necessary for the trial and punishment of such offenders, their accomplices, aiders and abettors.

2. *Be it further ordained,* That the said Judge shall appoint a day, as early as practicable, for holding the said court, and shall give notice of the time appointed to the Solicitor of the District and the Sheriff of the county, and shall direct the Sheriff to notify three or more Justices of the Peace to meet at the office of the County Court Clerk of said county, and issue a *venire* to attend the said court; and the Sheriff shall summons them to attend at the time appointed, at the Court House of the said county, and the Judge shall cause the Grand Jury to be drawn from the said *venire*, who shall serve as Grand Jurors, to pass upon any bill or bills which may be sent before them, and the remainder of the *venire* shall, unless excused by the court, serve as traverse jurors. The said court shall have power to order, if necessary, a further *venire* in said cases.

3. *Be it further ordained,* That the same rules and regulations shall govern the said court that are used at the regular terms, as to the duties of the Judge, the Soliciter, the Sheriff, and all others concerned in the said causes of trial, and all under the same pay, &c.

4. *Be it further ordained*, That this ordinance shall be in force from and after its ratification.

Passed and ratified in open Convention the 10th day of February, 1862.

W. N. EDWARDS,
Teste :   Pres. of Convention.
WALTER L. STEELE, Secretary,
L. C. EDWARDS, Ass't Secretary.

——

[No. 16.]
AN ORDINANCE GRANTING BOUNTY TO CERTAIN NORTH CAROLINA VOLUNTEERS.

1. *Be it ordained by the Delegates of the people of North Carolina in Convention assembled, and it is hereby ordained by the authority of the same*, That the volunteers from this State in the military service of the Confederacy, where North Carolina is or may be credited for the same by the Confederate Government, are justly entitled to, and should, therefore, receive the bounty authorized by the acts of the eighth day of May, A. D., 1861, and of the tenth day of May, 1861, whether the same volunteered first to the State or directly to the Confederate Government : *Provided, however,* That the officers of all volunteers directly to the Confederate States shall make such returns as the Governor may require.

2. *Be it further ordained*, That the Governor be authorized and requested to direct the paymaster to pay all volunteers who may not have received the same, such bounty as they are declared to be entitled to by the above section of this ordinance.

Passed and ratified in open Convention the 10th day of February, A. D., 1862.

W. N. EDWARDS,
Teste :   Pres. of Convention.
WALTER L. STEELE, Secretary,
L. C. EDWARDS, Assistant Secretary.

[No. 17.]

AN ORDINANCE SUPPLEMENTAL TO AN ORDI-
NANCE, RATIFIED AT THE PRESENT SESSION
OF THIS CONVENTION, ENTITLED "AN ORDI-
NANCE IN ADDITION TO AND AMENDMENT OF
AN ACT OF THE GENERAL ASSEMBLY, RATI-
FIED THE 15th DAY OF FEBRUARY, 1861, ENTI-
TLED AN ACT TO INCORPORATE THE CHATHAM
RAILROAD COMPANY, AND TO REPEAL AN ACT
SUPPLEMENTAL THERETO, RATIFIED THE 23rd
OF FEBRUARY, 1861," AND AUTHORIZING CER-
TAIN PERSONS TO OPEN BOOKS OF SUBSCRIP-
TION TO THE CAPITAL STOCK OF SAID COM-
PANY.

1. *Be it ordained by the Delegates of the people of North
Carolina in Convention assembled, and it is hereby ordained by
the authority of the same,* That an act of the General Assembly, entitled " An act to incorporate the Chatham Railroad
Company," be amended by adding to the section 2d, the following : " And a majority of said general commissioners shall
be competent to transact business; and in the mean time it
shall be lawful for books of subscription to said stock to be
opened in the city of Raleigh, under the direction of Geo. W.
Mordecai, William Henry Jones and Wm. W. Vass, or either
of them : in the town of Newbern, under the direction of Ed.
Stanly, A. T. Jerkins, W. H. Oliver, or any one of them : in
the town of Goldsboro', under the direction of E. A. Thomp-
son, Richard Washington, P. A. Wiley, or any one of them ;
at Pittsboro', under the direction of H. A. London, John H.
Haughton, John A. Womack, or any one of them ; at Haywood, under the direction of B. I. Howze, R. K. Smith and I.
N. Clegg, or any one of them ; at Warrenton, under the direction of J. B. Batchelor, John White, Richard T. Arrington, or
any one of them ; at Hillsboro', under the direction of William
A. Graham, Thomas Webb, P. B. Ruffin, or any one of them ;

at Smithfield, under the direction of J. W. B. Watson, Edwin Sanders, J. B. Beckwith, or any one of them; at Oxford, under the direction of S. S. Royster, C. H. K. Taylor, R. B. Gilliam, or any one of them; at Louisburg, under the direction of J. J. Davis, J. King, D. S. Hill, or any one of them; at Norfolk, under the direction of S. M. Wilson, Kader Biggs, Jas. Gordon, or any one of them; and at Petersburg, under the direction of W. T. Joynes, R. K. Martin and George D. Baskerville, or any one of them; and said general commissioners shall have power to appoint a Chairman of their body, Treasurer, and all other officers their organization may require, and to sue for and recover all sums of money that ought, under said act, to be recovered by them in the name of said corporation.

Passed and ratified in open Convention the 10th day of February, A. D., 1862.

W. N. EDWARDS,
Pres. of Convention.

Teste :

WALTER L. STEELE, Secretary,
L. C. EDWARDS, Assistant Secretary.

———

[No. 18.]
RESOLUTIONS RELATING TO RE-ENLISTMENT OF VOLUNTEERS.

Resolved, That in the opinion of this Convention, it is of the utmost importance, in the existing war, that our country shall not lose the services of the gallant volunteers of this State at the expiration of their present term of twelve months, and that such incentives to re-enlist should be held out to them as may induce their return to the army, after a brief interval for visiting their homes.

Resolved, That the Congress of the Confederate States should offer such inducements in bounties of money and public land, devolving to them from the United States, within the States of the Confederacy and in the territories; and in pensions, in case of death, disability, and long terms of service, to volunteers enlisting for the war, as will procure the return of those inured to the service, and shall prevail with others to follow their example in filling up the ranks of the army.

Resolved, That any volunteers of this State re-enlisting in the service as herein proposed, should have the privilege of choosing their company officers by companies, and their regimental field officers by the commissioned officers of companies. and in forming regiments, the companies heretofore associated should be kept together where they are filled up in convenient time, and any new companies should be added to the regiment having nearest its complement, when such new company shall be received into the service.

Resolved, That a copy of these resolutions be transmitted by the Secretary of this Convention to the Senators and Representatives of this State in the Confederate Congress, with a request that they bring the subject embraced in them to the consideration of Congress.

Passed and ratified in open Convention the 14th day of February, A. D., 1862.

W. N. EDWARDS,
Pres. of Convention.

Teste :

    WALTER L. STEELE, Secretary,

    L. C. EDWARDS, Ass't Secretary.

[No. 19.]

RESOLUTIONS CONCERNING THE MANUFACTURE OF SULPHUR AND SALTPETRE.

1. *Resolved*, That the Governor be requested, and he is hereby authorized to employ the necessary force and procure the necessary apparatus to manufacture Sulphur and Saltpetre for the use of the State, at such place or places, in or out of this

Stats, as he may deem proper, and that he draw upon the Treasury for the money to meet the expense thereof.

Resolved, That the Governor be requested to call upon the Government of the Confederate States for a supply of ammuition for our militia and other forces.

Passed and ratified in open Convention the 14th day of February, A. D., 1862.

W. N. EDWARDS,

Teste :   Pres. of Convention.

    WALTER L. STEELE, Secretary,

    L. C. EDWARDS, Ass't Secretary.

[No. 20.]

RESOLUTION TO RAISE CERTAIN ARTILLERY COMPANIES FOR THE DEFENCE OF WILMINGTON.

1. *Resolved,* That the Governor be, and he is hereby authorized to raise by volunteer enlistment, not exceeding three artillery companies to serve at the batteries already erected, or which may hereafter be erected on the Cape Fear River, below or at, and in the vicinity of the town of Wilmington, and that the men constituting such companies be entitled to the same bounty, pay and allowances as are by law allowed to the companies in the service of the Confederate States.

2. *Be it further resolved,* That the Governor be authorized to appoint Captains and Lieutenants to recruit such companies : the term of service of said companies to be for twelve months, or for three years or the war, unless sooner discharged by the Governor.   •

Passed and ratified in open Convention the 15th day of February, A. D., 1862.

F. B. SATTERTHWAITE,

Teste :   President *pro tem.*

    W. L. STEELE, Secretary,

    L. C. EDWARDS, Ass't Secretary.

[No. 21.]

AN ORDINANCE TO PROVIDE FOR THE ASSUMPTION AND PAYMENT OF THE CONFEDERATE TAX.

1. *Be it ordained by the Delegates of the people of North Carolina, in Convention assembled, and it is hereby ordained by the authority of the same,* That the State of North Carolina will, and doth hereby assume the payment of the tax known as the war tax, levied by the government of the Confederate States upon the people of North Carolina, by an act of the Confederate Congress, ratified on the —— day of ——, 1861.

2. *Be it further ordained,* That in order to provide the means for the payment of said tax, the Treasurer of the State is hereby directed to issue Treasury notes, redeemable in five years, to an amount not exceeding a sum sufficient to provide the payment of said tax, which notes shall be made convertible, at the option of the holder, into coupon bonds bearing seven per cent. interest, payable semi-annually, at the Treasury, and such bonds being redeemable ten years after date.

3. *Be it further ordained,* That the Public Treasurer is hereby directed, when called upon to do so, to issue the coupon bonds described in the preceding section of this ordinance for the purpose therein specified.

4. *Be it further ordained,* That the Treasurer is hereby directed to apply the Treasury notes to be issued in obedience to this ordinance, in such manner as may be necessary to the payment of said Confederate tax, which he is hereby directed to make.

5. *Be it further ordained,* That in payment of the Treasury notes hereby authorized, or of the bonds in which they are funded, the funds in the Treasury derived from the ordinary subjects of taxation, shall not be used, but the same shall be raised by a tax on the same subjects of taxation, with the same exemptions that are made in the act of the Confederate Congress imposing said tax, so that the white polls and persons

whose estates do not exceed five hundred dollars, shall not be liable to pay any part thereof; and those who have money in possession or in deposit, shall be liable as under said act of Congress.

6. *Be it further ordained,* That for the purposes of raising the money to pay said Treasury notes or bonds in which they may be funded, an additional tax list shall be made out, setting forth only the subjects of taxation enumerated in the said act of the Confederate Congress, and the Treasurer shall open and keep a separate account of said fund.

Passed and ratified in open Convention the 17th day of February, A. D., 1862.

WILL. A. GRAHAM,
President pro tem.

Teste:

WALTER L. STEELE, Secretary.

L. C. EDWARDS, Ass't Secretary.

[No. 22.]

A RESOLUTION IN FAVOR OF SOLDIERS DETAINED AT RAILROAD STATIONS IN THIS STATE.

Resolved, That the Quartermaster and Commissary at Raleigh and other railroad connections in this State be directed, if in their power, to furnish all volunteers who may be necessarily detained at these places, with food and lodging so long as they are necessarily detained, and they shall be allowed the same in the settlement of their accounts.

Passed and ratified in open Convention the 17th day of February, A. D., 1862.

F. B. SATTERTHWAITE,
President pro tem.

Teste:

W. L. STEELE, Secretary,

L. C. EDWARDS, Ass't Secretary.

AN ORDINANCE TO RAISE NORTH CAROLINA'S QUOTA OF CONFEDERATE TROOPS.

1. *Be it ordained by the Delegates of the people of North Carolina in Convention assembled, and it is hereby ordained by the authority of the same,* That it shall be the duty of the Governor, from time to time, to issue his proclamation calling for volunteers to meet the requisitions of the Confederate Government, now made, or hereafter to be made: *Provided, however,* That volunteers heretofore in service, re-enlisting, shall have credit for the time they have served: *Provided, further,* That said volunteers shall not be for a longer time than three years, and to be sooner discharged in case the present war terminates before the expiration of that time: *And, provided further,* That the Governor shall not be required to keep in the Confederate service more than the regular quota of North Carolina.

2. *Be it further ordained,* That the Governor shall call upon the counties to furnish, by volunteering, the necessary number of troops, under the present requisition, according to white population (after crediting them with the troops already in the service, for three years or the war, and the volunteers for twelve months) to complete their respective quotas, on or before the 15th of March, 1862.

3. *Be it further ordained,* That the Governor shall require each Captain now in the service, on or before the 15th day of March, 1862, to return to the Adjutant General a list of the officers and men under his command, with the county of the residence of each at the time of his entry into service.

4. *Be it further ordained,* That the Governor shall call upon the several captains of volunteer companies from North Carolina in the field for twelve months, or officers in command of companies, to muster their companies for re-enlistment, and shall make known to them the earnest desire of this Convention and the people of North Carolina, that they shall enlist for three years or the war, and in order to forward this purpose,

the captains of companies or officers in command of the company, on the occasion of such muster, shall put the question distinctly to every officer and soldier belonging thereto, whether he will re-enlist for three years or the war, or not; and those agreeing so to re-enlist, he will cause to subscribe a roll containing such obligation, with their names and places of residence at the times of their first entry into service, and the signatures of the persons so re-enlisting shall be as binding as if they had been mustered into service; which lists he will immediately return to the office of the Adjutant General of the State.

5. *Be it further ordained*, That volunteer companies now in service, re-enlisting, may retain their present organization, or re-organize at their option; and that all volunteers not re-enlisting with present organization, shall be thrown into companies and proceed to elect company commissioned officers, who shall be commissioned by the Governor; and the company commissioned officers shall elect their field officers: *Provided, however*, That the commissions of all officers, company or field, who shall be re-elected, shall bear the dates of their former commissions.

6. *Be it further ordained*, That the Governor shall have power to appoint captains and lieutenants to recruit men for the service aforesaid, and to organize the men so recruited into companies and regiments; and the company commissioned officers shall, in all cases, elect their field officers under the rules now prescribed: *Provided, however*, That no person shall receive a commission or pay under said appointments, except as follows: When any person shall tender forty privates, who in writing have agreed to serve under him, a Captain's commission and pay; and in like manner for twenty-five privates, a first Lieutenant's commission and pay; and for fifteen privates a second Lieutenant's commission and pay.

7. *Be it further ordained*, That a bounty of fifty dollars, deducting the bounty already paid, shall be paid by the State to all privates, musicians, and non-commissioned officers whose

term of service altogether shall be for three years or the war,
to be paid at the following times, to-wit: To all volunteers now
in service at the time of their re-entry into service ; to all now
in the service for three years or the war, at the expiration of
their first year's service ; to all new volunteers, at the time of
their entry into service : *Provided, however,* That any soldier
may permit his bounty to remain in the Treasury and draw the
same, with interest, at the expiration of one year from the
time it is due, or at the time of his discharge : *And, provided
further,* That such payment may be made in Treasury notes,
unless otherwise provided by law.

Passed and ratified in open Convention the 19th day of February, A. D., 1862.

                              W. N. EDWARDS,
Teste :   Pres. of Convention.
    WALTER L. STEELE, Secretary,
    L. C. EDWARDS, Ass't Secretary.

———

[No. 24.]
AN ORDINANCE TO PROHIBIT, FOR A LIMITED
TIME, THE MANUFACTURE OF SPIRITUOUS LI-.
QUORS FROM GRAIN.

1. *Be it ordained by the Delegates of the people of North Carolina in Convention assembled, and it is hereby ordained by the
authority of the same,* That there shall be a tax of thirty cents
levied on each gallon of spiritous liquors manufactured in this
State, out of any corn, wheat, rye or oats, or any mixture of
any or either of them, from the ratification of this ordinance
up to the fifteenth day of April next.

2. *Be it further ordained,* That from and after the fifteenth
day of April next, it shall not be lawful for any person in this
State to distil any such spirituous liquors, and all persons
guilty of violating this section of this ordinance shall, for each

and every act of distillation, be guilty of a misdemeanor, and on conviction thereof, shall be fined or imprisoned at the discretion of the court; the fine not to be less than one hundred dollars, or the imprisonment less than thirty days.

3. *Be it further ordained*, That there shall be levied a tax of one dollar on every gallon of spirituous liquors sold in this State, not of the manufacture of this State; and said tax shall be paid by the seller, and should the seller be a non-resident, then the tax shall be paid by the purchaser.

4. *Be it further ordained*, That each and every person, when he gives in his list of taxable property, shall also give in, on oath, to the magistrate taking said list, the number of gallons of spirituous liquors on which he is liable to pay taxes under the provisions of this ordinance, under the penalties, liabilities and forfeitures already provided by law in such cases.

5. *Be it further ordained*, That the tax of one dollar, mentioned in section third of this ordinance, shall not apply to liquors brought into this State before the first day of March next.

6. *Be it further ordained*, That this ordinance shall be in force from and after its ratification, and continue in force until the first day of January, 1863, and no longer, unless re-enacted, modified or amended by the General Assembly.

Passed and ratified in open Convention the 21st day of February, A. D., 1862.

W. N. EDWARDS,
Teste :　　　　　　　　　　　　　　　　Pres. of Convention.
WALTER L. STEELE, Secretary,
L. C. EDWARDS, Ass't Secretary.

———

[No. 25.]

AN ORDINANCE RELATIVE TO THE EXPENSES INCURRED BY THE BOARD OF CLAIMS.

Be it ordained by the delegates of the people of North Carolina in Convention assembled, and it is hereby ordained by the authority of the same, That the Board of Claims may draw upon the Public Treasurer for all incidental expenses necessarily incurred by them in the discharge of their official duties : *Provided,* That such expenses shall not exceed, in the whole, the sum of five hundred dollars : *And, provided further,* That said Board shall, in their final account, render to the State a statement of all monies by them expended under this ordinance.

Passed and ratified in open Convention the 21st day of February, A. D., 1862.

                              W. N. EDWARDS,
Teste :   Pres. of Convention.
      WALTER L. STEELE, Secretary,
      L. C. EDWARDS, Assistant Secretary.

————

[No. 26.]

AN ORDINANCE TO MAKE SOME PROVISION FOR THE FAMILIES OF SOLDIERS DYING IN SERVICE.

1. *Be it ordained by the delegates of the people of North Carolina in Convention assembled, and it is hereby ordained by the authority of the same,* That in case of the death in service of any soldier, intestate, who, at the time of his death was, or shall be, entitled to bounty or any arrearages of pay from this State, such bounty and pay shall belong and be payable to the widow of such intestate soldier, and if there be no widow, to his children, and if there be no children, then to his next of kin as designated in the Statute of Distributions, and in the proportions therein prescribed, and the identity of the person or persons claiming the same, and the degree of relationship of him, her or them, to the intestate as aforesaid, shall be established to the satisfaction of the proper executive or military authorities, according to such regulations and rules as may be prescribed by the said authorities.

2. *Be it further ordained*, That any person who shall wilfully swear falsely in any affidavit, deposition or testimony made or given for the purpose of establishing or endeavoring to establish a claim to any such bounty or pay, shall be guilty of perjury, and upon conviction thereof shall be punished accordingly.

Passed and ratified in open Convention the 22d day of February, 1862.

W. N. EDWARDS,
Pres. of Convention.

Teste:
WALTER L. STEELE, Secretary,
L. C. EDWARDS, Ass't Secretary.

[No. 27.]
AN ORDINANCE CONCERNING THE PAYMASTER'S DEPARTMENT.

1. *Be it ordained by the delegates of the people of North Carolina in Convention assembled, and it is hereby ordained by the authority of the same*, That the twenty-third section of the act of the last session of the General Assembly, entitled "Militia Bill," be amended as follows: "That there shall be one additional officer appointed by the Governor, to be attached as Assistant to the Paymaster's Department, with the rank and pay of a First Lieutenant, who shall be subject to the same chief of the said department, and to the rules and regulations of the same.

2. *Be it further ordained*, That the said office, created by this ordinance, may be vacated by the Governor or the Legislature, whenever the public interest may require.

Passed and ratified in open Convention the 24th day of February, A. D., 1862.

W. N. EDWARDS,
Pres. of Convention.

Teste:
WALTER L. STEELE, Secretary,
L. C. EDWARDS, Assistant Secretary.

[No. 28.]
RESOLUTION IN BEHALF OF WILLIAM R. LOVELL.

Resolved, That the Treasurer of the State pay to William R. Lovell the sum of eighty-two dollars, expended by him for the use of the sick soldiers of the eleventh regiment of North Carolina Volunters, near Manassas, when employed as a nurse in August and September last.

Passed and ratified in open Convention the 25th day of February, A. D., 1862.

                        W. N. EDWARDS,
Teste :   Pres. of Convention.
WALTER L. STEELE, Secretary,
L. C. EDWARDS, Ass't Secretary.

[No. 29.]
A RESOLUTION IN FAVOR OF THE DOORKEEPERS.

Resolved, That the Treasurer pay to the Doorkeepers of the Convention twenty-five dollars each, for servants' hire and extra expenses incurred by them during the present session.

Read, passed and ratified in open Convention the 24th day of February, A. D., 1862.

                        W. N. EDWARDS,
Teste :   Pres. of Convention.
WALTER L. STEELE, Secretary,
L. C. EDWARDS, Assistant Secretary.

[No. 30.]
AN ORDINANCE TO ENCOURAGE THE MANUFAC-TURE OF COTTON AND WOOL CARDS.

Be it ordained by the delegates of the people of North Carolina, in Convention assembled, and it is hereby ordained by the authority of the same, That if any person or persons shall erect buildings and construct machinery, for the purpose of manufacturing cotton and wool cards, and shall make proof to the Governor of the cost of such works, the Governor be, and he is hereby authorized to draw on the Treasurer for sums not exceeding the cost of said works, to be loaned to the owners thereof, on the execution by them of bonds payable to the State, with sufficient security, conditioned to repay such sums at such time as the General Assembly may prescribe, and with such interest as may be required, not exceeding six per cent. per annum : *Provided,* That such advances shall not exceed, in the aggregate, the sum of ten thousand dollars : *And, provided further,* That the cards thus manufactured shall, in the first place, be offered to sale to the citizens of this State.

Passed and ratified in open Convention the 25th day of February, A. D., 1862.

W. N. EDWARDS,
Pres. of Convention.

Teste :

> W. L. STEELE, Secretary,
> L. C. EDWARDS, Ass't Secretary.

[No. 31.]

AN ORDINANCE FOR THE PAYMENT OF CLAIMS AUDITED AND ALLOWED BY THE BOARD OF CLAIMS.

1. *Be it ordained by the delegates of the people of North Carolina, in Convention assembled, and it is hereby ordained by the authority of the same,* That the Public Treasurer, upon the warrant of the Governor, pay to Samuel L. Dill, of Carteret, the sum of thirteen hundred dollars ; to G. W. Dill & Co., of Carteret, fourteen hundred and thirty-three dollars and thirty-three cents; to W. G. Towler, of New Hanover, thirty-two dollars and fifty cents ; to the Marine Railway Company, of New Hanover, forty-eight dollars and ten cents ; to Dr. Jno.

F. Miller, High Point, forty dollars and ninety cents; to Mc-
Intyre & Brown, New Hanover, sixty-eight dollars and twenty-
six cents; to Thomas H. Allen, of Craven, fifty-seven dollars;
to J. M. M. Houston & Co., Lincoln, one hundred and four
dollars and fifty-seven cents; to John M. Wolfe, Orange, three
dollars and fifty cents; to E. H. Cunningham, Buncombe, one
hundred and forty-three dollars and twenty-five cents; to
Willie Walston, Edgecombe, forty-six dollars and sixty-five
cents; to P. B. Hardin & Co., Alamance, eight dollars and
thirty-five cents; to Dr. W. D. Somers, White Sulphur Spings,
Va., five dollars and seventy-five cents; to E. J. Hale & Sons,
Cumberland, five dollars and thirty cents; to J. H. Wood,
Rowan, two hundred and fifty-eight dollars and forty-eight
cents; to John A. Graves, Caswell, twelve dollars and sixty
cents; to H. C. Stroud, assignee for Frank Harris, Orange,
thirty dollars; to Harris & Howell, New Hanover, sixty dollars; to Philip Sale, Greenville County, Va., twenty-five dollars; to Joseph Barnham, Northampton, seven dollars; to Phifer
& York, Cabarrus, one thousand and thirty-nine dollars and
sixty-seven cents; to Samuel Calvert, Northampton, one hundred and fifty dollars; to W. P. Lloyd, Edgecombe, ninety-six
dollars and seventy-five cents; to Edwin M. Holt, Alamance,
two hundred and eighty dollars and thirty-two cents; to Jas.
Tiddy, Lincoln, forty dollars; to William Tiddy, Lincoln, four
dollars; to John L. Bridgers, Edgecombe, thirty-five dollars
and fifty-five cents; to D. C. McGregor, Buncombe, six dollars and twenty-five cents; to W. H. Stone, Buncombe, fifty-
nine dollars and twenty-five cents; to R. S. Alexander, Buncombe, thirty-three dollars and three cents; to S. H. Christian,
Montgomery, thirty-four dollars and seventy-five cents; to Isaac
Ramsey, Carteret, ninety-six dollars and eighty-four cents; to
Isaac Ramsey, assignee for L. H. Styron, Carteret, fifteen dollars and sixty cents; to Jos. S. Norman, Washington, thirty-
three dollars; to Dr. Peter E. Hines, Craven, one hundred and
two dollars and sixty cents; to Dr. A. C. Folson, Brunswick,
ninety dollars; to J. R. and W. B. Cainer, Martin, forty-six
dollars and thirty-eight cents; to Dunn & Spencer, Petersburg,

one hundred and thirty-three dollars and seventy-six (cents) dollars ; to Fulton & Price, New Hanover, twenty-two dollars and fifty cents ; to Hart & Baily, New Hanover, two hundred and sixty-eight dollars and fifty-eight cents ; to John P. Mabry, Davidson, twenty dollars and twenty cents ; to J. B. White-hurst, Carteret, twenty-four dollars ; to Thomas Duncan & Son, Carteret, eighty-three dollars and seventeen cents ; to E. G. Clark, Wilson, fifty dollars and twenty-five cents ; to Mrs. Sarah A. Reid, Wake, thirty-five dollars ; to Patton & Alex-ander, Buncombe, two hundred and forty-three dollars and forty cents ; to A. Mitchell & Son, Craven, two hundred and fifty dollars and twenty-five cents ; to W. W. Smith, Bun-combe, two hundred and thirty-five dollars and sixty-one cents ; to Benjamin M. Walker, Washington, one hundred and twenty-eight dollars and ninety cents ; to J. F. Crawley, Beaufort, one hundred and thirty-eight dollars and fifty-five cents ; to Capt. C. M. Avery, Burke, forty-two dollars and fifty cents ; to Do-zier & Co., Edgecombe, eighty-one dollars and thirty-five cents ; to Jacob Bachman, Chowan, twenty-four dollars and thirty-five cents ; to J. L. Pennington, Craven, seventy-seven dollars and forty-three cents ; to E. G. Mangum & Co., Orange, one hun-dred and eight dollars and thirty-nine cents ; to W. C. King, Carteret, two hundred and fifty-eight dollars and eighty cents ; to Geo. W. Ward, Martin, twenty-five dollars ; to W. W. Hap-per, Halifax, fifty dollars and thirty cents ; to J. J. Jenkins, Cleveland, twenty-six dollars and thirty-three cents ; to Miller & Foster, Davidson, three hundred and forty-two dollars and twenty-eight cents ; to James A. Washington, Wayne, five hundred and ninety-one dollars and fifty-nine cents ; to Rich'd C. Coher, Northampton, forty-five dollars ; to J. R. Davidson, Iredell, forty-six dollars and ninety-three cents ; to Polk county, five hundred and one dollars and twenty-eight cents ; to Richmond county, three thousand three hundred and nine-teen dollars and thirty-one cents ; to Alamance county, two thousand six hundred and ninety-one dollars and fifty-four cents ; to Iredell county, two thousand one hundred and forty-nine dollars and eighty-six cents ; to Macon county, six hun-

dred and fifty-four dollars and seventy-five cents; to Currituck
county, eighty-nine dollars and ninety-one cents; to Cumberland county, five thousand four hundred and thirty-seven dollars and sixty-six cents; to Alexander county, five hundred
and twelve dollars and eleven cents; to Lenoir county, six
thousand four hundred and ninety-nine dollars and nine cents;
to Joseph H. Neff, New Hanover, one hundred and sixty-three
dollars and sixty cents; to Jerry Drew, and others, Northampton, one hundred dollars; to Stanly county, two thousand seven
hundred and thirty-three dollars and thirty-five cents; to Surry
county, two thousand eight hundred and fifty-three dollars and
thirty-one cents; to Caswell county, three thousand nine hundred and forty-three dollars and fifty-seven cents; to Charles
M. Rogers, one hundred and eighty-five dollars and sixty-five
cents; and to Charles H. K. Taylor, assignee, three hundred
and twenty-two dollars and sixty-nine cents; and that said payments be made without prejudice to claims which have been
presented and not allowed, on account of commutation pay received from the Confederate States.

Passed and ratified in open Convention the 25th day of February, A. D., 1862.

                                    W. N. EDWARDS,
Teste :   Pres. of Convention.
    WALTER L. STEELE, Secretary,
    L. C. EDWARDS, Assistant Secretary.

———

[No. 32.]
AN ORDINANCE TO TAX MONEY.

1. *Be it ordained by the Delegates of the people of North
Carolina in Convention assembled, and it is hereby ordained by
the authority of the same,* That hereafter all monies on hand,
and all monies on deposit with individuals, or in the banks or
other corporations, shall be taxed one-fifth of one per cent., as

now imposed on money at interest; and all persons having
money in possession or on deposit, as aforesaid, on the first day
of April in each and every year, shall be required to list the
same when they list other taxable property, under the same liabilities and responsibilities as are now imposed by law for failure
or neglect to list other taxable property: *Provided*, That bank
notes and Confederate State Treasury notes shall be considered
money.

2. *Be it further ordained*, That the provisions of this ordinance shall not apply to those who may have less than one
hundred dollars to list.

3. *Be it further ordained*, That this ordinance may be modified or repealed by the General Assembly.

Passed and ratified in open Convention the 26th day
of February, A. D., 1862.

W. N. EDWARDS,

Teste :   ,   Pres. of Convention.
   WALTER L. STEELE, Secretary,
   L. C. EDWARDS, Assistant Secretary.

[No. 33.]

AN ORDINANCE REGULATING THE APPOINTMENT
OF COMPANY OFFICERS.

*Be it ordained by the Delegates of the people of North Caro-
lina, in Convention assembled, and it is hereby ordained by the
authority of the same,* That whenever a vacancy occurs in the
commissioned officers of any of the companies in this State,
raised under an act entitled " an act to raise ten thousand State
Troops," or to be raised under the ordinance entitled " an ordinance to raise North Carolina's quota of Troops," the vacancy shall be filled by promotion of the officers next in grade in
in said company ; and whenever a vacancy shall occur in the
office of junior second Lieutenant, the vacancy shall be filled by

election by the non-commissioned officers and privates of the company in which such vacancy occurs.

Passed and ratified in open Convention the 26th day of February, A. D., 1862.

W. N. EDWARDS,
Pres. of Convention.

Teste :
WALTER L. STEELE, Secretary,
L. C. EDWARDS, Ass't Secretary.

[No. 34.]

AN ORDINANCE CONFERRING ON THE COMMISSIONERS OF TOWN OF WILMINGTON AND OTHER TOWNS CERTAIN POWERS FOR THE DEFENCE THEREOF.

1. *Be it ordained, &c.*, That the commissioners of the town of Wilmington shall have power to place obstructions in the river, and to erect or to complete, if already in process of erection, any work or works upon, or at the mouth of Cape Fear River, or around, near or within the said town, which they may deem necessary for the defence thereof, and also for the like purpose, to purchase cannon, powder, ball and other munitions of war : *Provided*, That the said obstructions are placed in the river, with the consent of the Confederate officer in command.

2. *Be it further ordained*, That to meet the expenses which may be incurred under the foregoing section, the said commissioners shall have power to borrow money upon such terms and under such regulations as they may adopt, and to impose such taxes upon the subjects now liable to taxation within said town as may be necessary.

3. *Be it further ordained*, That whenever the commanding officer shall certify that the expenses incurred by the commissioners under this ordinance were necessary for the State defence, the same shall be a charge upon the Public Treasury : *Provided,*

That application shall have first been made to the Confederate Government, and they shall have failed to assume the payment of the same six months after said application.

4. *Be it further ordained,* That the provisions of this ordinance be extended to the commissioners of the towns of Newbern and Washington, or any other towns that may make the same application, under similar circumstances.

Passed and ratified in open Convention the 26th day of February, A. D., 1862.

W. N. EDWARDS,
Pres. of Convention.

Teste :

WALTER L. STEELE, Secretary,
L. C. EDWARDS, Ass't Secretary.

———

[No. 35.]

AN ORDINANCE TO PROVIDE FOR FUNDING THE TREASURY NOTES OF THIS STATE, AND FOR OTHER PURPOSES.

1. *Be it ordained, &c.,* That any of the Treasury notes issued or hereafter to be issued under the ordinance of this Convention, ratified the 1st of December, 1861, directing the issue of three millions of Treasury notes, as well as those issued by an ordinance of the present session, entitled "An ordinance to provide for the assumption and payment of the Confederate Tax," may be funded at the will of the holder in coupon bonds of the State, to be prepared by the Treasurer, and payable 20 years after date, or sooner, at the pleasure of the State, and bearing interest at the rate of eight per cent. per annum, payable semi-annually at the Treasury, or in six per cent. bonds of the State, payable 30 years after the 1st of January, 1862, interest payable semi-annually, exchangeable in Treasury notes, at the option of the holder, from time to time, until the Treasury notes fall due, said bonds being of the denominations of $500 and $1,000, in equal proportions.

2. *Be it further ordained*, That all taxes due to the State or to counties, and for 'school purposes, or taxes for the poor, and all payments for entries of public lands, and all other dues to the State, and all fines and forfeitures for the use of the State or counties, shall be paid in Treasury notes of the State or of the Confederate States, or in the notes of such of the solvent banks of this State as shall receive and continue to receive and pay out as money at par the Treasury notes of this State, or in gold or silver coin; and it shall be the duty of the Treasurer to issue instructions to the Sheriffs and tax collectors in the several counties on this subject, and it shall not be lawful for any Sheriff or collector to receive taxes in any other funds than as directed by the Treasurer under this ordinance.

3. *Be it further ordained*, That all the Treasury notes funded in bonds, or paid into the Treasury for taxes or other public dues, may be re-issued in payment of the debts of the State, or in exchange for six per cent. bonds of the State, on application of the holder at any time before the notes fall due: *Provided*, That the Treasury notes issued to pay the Confederate tax shall not be used to pay the debts of the State; and the Treasurer and Comptroller shall each keep an account of all notes re-issued and those refunded in bonds, from time to time, and the date of such transaction, and particularly noting the interest on each bond when taken up, and the amount of interest due on each bond when exchanged for Treasury notes, and in all cases shall charge the party receiving such bonds with the interest due at the time of delivery.

4. *Be it further ordained*, That as the exigencies of the public service may, in the opinion of the Governor, require before the first day of January, 1863, the Public Treasurer is authorized and required to issue other Treasury notes as aforesaid, not exceeding, in amount, the further sum of fifteen hundred thousand dollars, and that the said notes shall be prepared, signed and issued as in the said ordinance, ratified on the first day of December, 1861.

☞ 5. *Be it further ordained,* That the aggregate amount of said Treasury notes outstanding at any one time, and of the bonds given in exchange for or discharge of Treasury notes as aforesaid, shall not exceed the amount of such notes authorized by law heretofore, or in this ordinance.

6. *Be it further ordained,* That it shall be the duty of the Treasurer, as soon as convenient, to issue Treasury notes of the denominations of five, ten and twenty dollars in equal amounts, instead of, and to exchange for, any of the Treasury notes heretofore issued, not bearing interest, of the denominations of fifty and one hundred dollars, on the application of the holders of said notes, and when so taken up or exchanged, the said notes of fifty and one hundred dollars shall be cancelled, and the same shall be noted by the Treasurer on his books and on the books of the Comptroller.

7. *Be it further ordained,* That if any one shall falsely forge, or knowingly pass, or offer to pass, any false, forged, or counterfeited paper, purporting to be a Treasurer note or bond of this State, he shall be liable to indictment in the Superior Courts in the county in which such offence may be committed, and on conviction thereof, shall suffer all the pains and penalties, according to the 59th section of the 34th chapter of the Revised Code.

8. *Be it further ordained,* That in addition to the Treasury notes heretofore ordered to be issued, it shall be the duty of the Treasurer to issue one million of dollars, in small denominations, to-wit: four hundred thousand dollars in the denomination of two dollars, four hundred thousand dollars in the denomination of one dollar, one hundred thousand dollars in the denomination of fifty cents, fifty thousand dollars in the denomination of twenty-five cents, twenty-five thousand dollars in the denomination of twenty cents, and twenty-five thousand dollars in the denomination of ten cents, payable on the first day of January, 1866, to be used in liquidation of any claims against the State to persons willing to receive the same, but not to be funded in bonds of the State, but shall be receiv-

8

able in payment of taxes or other public dues; and he shall keep an accurate account of the issues, from time to time, made under this section of this ordinance.

9. *Be it further ordained,* That no bank receiving the Treasury notes of this State, as contemplated in the second section of this ordinance, shall be required to receive, or have on hand at any one time, more than two-fifths of the capital stock of such bank in said notes.

10. *Be it further ordained,* That so much of the act of the General Assembly, entitled "An act to provide ways and means for the defence of the State," ratified September 18th, 1861, as authorizes the issue of one million dollars of the denominations of two dollars, one dollar, fifty cents, twenty-five cents, twenty cents, ten cents and five cents, and also the ordinance of the Convention, ratified December 1, 1861, directing the issue of three millions of dollars of Treasury notes, and the ordinance to provide for the assumption and payment of the Confederate tax, as well as all the issues of Treasury notes and bonds under said act and ordinances, are hereby ratified and confirmed.

11. *Be it further ordained,* That in the event of the inability of the Public Treasurer or Comptroller to sign the Treasury notes authorized by law to be issued as speedily as the demands on the Treasury may require, then it shall be lawful for either of them to employ some discreet person, by and with the advice and consent of the Governor, to sign and countersign the said notes, whose names shall be published in the newspapers in the city of Raleigh.

12. *Be it further ordained,* That this ordinance may be repealed or modified by the General Assembly, but so as not to affect any transactions had or rights vested under the same, previous to such modification or repeal.

Read three times and ratified in open Convention the 26th day of February, A. D., 1862.

W. N. EDWARDS,
Pres. of Convention.

Teste:

WALTER L. STEELE, Secretary,
L. C. EDWARDS, Ass't Secretary.